How and why do people copy animals?

Bobbie Kalman

🌱 Crabtree Publishing Company

www.crabtreebooks.com

Dedicated by Samantha Crabtree
For Damian Jr. Galvin
You stole my heart with your big baby blues.
Love you my little Romeo, Aunty Sam.

Author and editor-in-chief
Bobbie Kalman

Publishing plan research and development
Reagan Miller

Editor
Kathy Middleton

Proofreader
Crystal Sikkens

Design
Bobbie Kalman
Katherine Berti
Samantha Crabtree (logo)

Photo research
Bobbie Kalman

Prepress technician
Samara Parent

Print and production coordinator
Margaret Amy Salter

Illustrations and photographs
Barbara Bedell: page 5 (middle)
Bigstockphoto: page 19 (top left)
Thinkstock: page 4 (both); page 6 (top); page 16
Shutterstock: Iurii Osadchi: page 17 (top);
　　Dinozzaver: page 17 (bottom); cover and all other photographs

Library and Archives Canada Cataloguing in Publication

Kalman, Bobbie, author
　　How and why do people copy animals? / Bobbie Kalman.

(All about animals close-up)
Includes index.
Issued in print and electronic formats.
ISBN 978-0-7787-1465-1 (bound).--ISBN 978-0-7787-1472-9 (pbk.).--
ISBN 978-1-4271-7637-0 (pdf).--ISBN 978-1-4271-7631-8 (html)

　　1. Bionics--Juvenile literature. I. Title.

Q320.5.K35 2015　　　　j003'.5　　　　C2014-908186-3
　　　　　　　　　　　　　　　　　　　　　　C2014-908187-1

Library of Congress Cataloging-in-Publication Data

Kalman, Bobbie, author.
　How and why do people copy animals? / Bobbie Kalman.
　　pages cm. -- (All about animals close-up)
　Includes index.
　ISBN 978-0-7787-1465-1 (reinforced library binding : alk. paper) --
ISBN 978-0-7787-1472-9 (pbk. : alk. paper) --
ISBN 978-1-4271-7637-0 (electronic pdf : alk. paper) --
ISBN 978-1-4271-7631-8 (electronic html : alk. paper)
　1. Animal behavior--Juvenile literature. 2. Human-animal relationships--
Juvenile literature. I. Title.

　QL751.5.K3364 2015
　591.5--dc23
　　　　　　　　　　　　　　　2014048908

Crabtree Publishing Company

www.crabtreebooks.com　　　1-800-387-7650

Printed in Canada/042015/BF20150203

Published in Canada
Crabtree Publishing
616 Welland Ave.
St. Catharines, Ontario
L2M 5V6

Published in the United States
Crabtree Publishing
PMB 59051
350 Fifth Avenue, 59th Floor
New York, New York 10118

Published in the United Kingdom
Crabtree Publishing
Maritime House
Basin Road North, Hove
BN41 1WR

Published in Australia
Crabtree Publishing
3 Charles Street
Coburg North
VIC 3058

Contents

Why copy animals?

Animals are able to adapt, or change to suit, the **habitats** in which they live. They find new ways to move, find food, and keep warm or cool in different kinds of **climate**. They adapt to the changes in their lives to stay alive. People also adapt to make their lives easier. They have learned many of the things they do from animals.

Long ago, people dressed in the furs of animals to keep warm. Today, people dress in animal costumes for fun. They also copy animal fur patterns on some clothes they design (see page 12).

Flying like birds

Flying takes birds from one place to another much faster than walking or running. People watched birds and wanted to fly too, so they could travel more quickly. They invented airplanes by copying birds. Airplanes changed people's lives.

People watched birds to learn how to fly so they could travel more quickly, too. This is how the airplane was invented. Where is the farthest place you have flown?

What do you think?

Why could the early airplane above not stay in the air for long, but the one on the right can?

Copying their moves

People learned to fly and **glide** by copying birds. They also copied other ways that animals move. People walk, run, hop, crawl, jump, leap, climb, and swim. Which animals move in these ways?

One girl is leaping over another. Which animal are they copying?

This girl has climbed a tree and is hanging by her arms and legs the way the raccoon above is doing. What other animals can do this?

fin

flipper

wet suit

flipper on diver

mask and snorkel

Moving in water

Dolphins have fins and flippers for swimming. This diver also has flippers. His **wet suit** keeps him warm the way a dolphin's skin keeps a dolphin warm.

What do you think?

How do flippers help people swim? What do divers wear to breathe underwater and see where they are going?

Hard shells to hard hats

Box turtles can pull their heads and legs into their shells. These turtles can then close their shells by pulling the bottom part up.

Turtles and tortoises have shells made of hard bone covered by **keratin**. Our fingernails are made of keratin. The shells cover the body parts of these animals. Some turtles can pull their heads and legs into their shells for even more protection.

This boy's football helmet protects his head the way a turtle shell protects a turtle's body. Why is it important to protect your head and body while playing sports such as football?

metal helmet
used in war
long ago

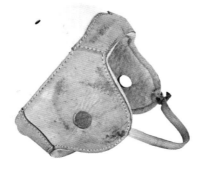

old football helmet
made of leather

helmet used
for skiing

People make helmets to protect their heads. The first helmets were made of heavy metal or leather. Today, most helmets are made of human-made materials such as plastic. People wear helmets while riding bicycles and motorcycles and when they play sports such as football, hockey, and baseball.

bike
helmets

What do you think?

What kinds of helmets do you wear?
Which helmet looks most like a turtle?

9

Spider silk and webs

Not all spiders build webs, but they all spin silk. Some spin as many as six kinds! Spiders use the silk to escape from danger, build homes, and trap **prey**. Spider silk is strong, stretchy, and does not break, even in very hot or cold temperatures. Some spider silk is five times as strong as steel!

Web-weaving spiders catch prey in their sticky webs. This spider has wrapped a bug in its silk. It will shoot a liquid into it, which will turn the insides of the bug to juice. The spider will then suck up the liquid and leave behind the bug's empty shell.

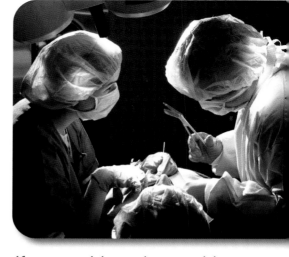

If we could produce spider silk, doctors could use it to make new body parts or sew up people with thin, strong stitches after surgery.

These children are on a climber that looks like a spiderweb. Children love playing on these climbing webs! They are great exercise and lots of fun!

What do you think?

If you could use spider silk, list three ways you would use it. Draw some spiderweb designs for a costume or decoration.

Copying coverings

Some animals, such as leopards, have beautiful fur. Many designs used on the clothes people wear are copied from animal coverings. Children especially love dressing up to look and act like animals.

People have hunted leopards to make coats from their fur. Today, most people will not wear fur coats because they do not want these animals killed, but they do copy the patterns.

This girl is wearing a dress with a leopard-print pattern. It is not made from fur.

what do you think?

The makeup on this boy's face looks like a tiger's face. The boy is also copying a tiger's roar. The girl has butterfly wings. Which animal do you like to copy? Why?

This baby is wearing a white snowsuit. How is its covering like the polar bear's?

Animal communities

One of the most important ways of life that people share with animals is living together in family groups and **communities**. Animals that are part of groups help one another find food, keep safe, and care for their young. Some animal groups hunt together, some build homes, and others take turns watching for **predators**.

Both people and animals enjoy spending time together in groups.

Prairie dogs teach their young the way people teach their children. They show their pups, or babies, how to find food, dig tunnels, and guard their communities from predators.

What can these students learn at school that prairie dogs cannot learn?

What do you think?

Animals must learn to communicate with their group members. How do you communicate with your family and friends?

Following the group

Both animals and people gather in large groups. Animals look for food or run from predators with their groups. Animals and people also bully one another in groups. They stop others from joining in certain activities or hurt them in other ways.

These snow monkeys spend much of their time keeping warm in this hot pool in Japan, but only the monkeys in the "ingroup" are welcome. The monkey sitting on the rock is not allowed to join the others in the pool.

People gather in crowds to watch sports, celebrate holidays, or just have fun. They also gather in crowds to **protest** laws and events that they want changed in their community or country.

Two girls are using words to bully another girl. Their words make her feel sad. How are the girls like the monkeys on page 16? What could the boy do to help stop the bullies?

What do you think?

How and when do you follow the crowd? How can following the crowd sometimes hurt others?

17

Building homes

Homes protect us from bad weather and keep us safe. Animals also build homes for **shelter** and to keep safe. How did people copy the homes of some animals?

People long ago had no machines for building homes. They lived in caves the way bears and other animals do.

These coyote pups live in a cave.
Which other animals live in caves?

Many birds make nests in trees.
Some make them on water.

How is the treehouse above
and the houseboat below
like nests built by birds?

19

Animals copy people, too!

Pets and many other animals are trained by people. Some animals take part in shows and learn to do tricks that people teach them to do. Some animals copy the actions of people and seem to have fun doing it. What kinds of things have you seen animals do?

How do cats and dogs celebrate their birthdays? Do you think they sing and take pictures? Why or why not?

Does this mouse know how to use a computer mouse?

Can this monkey really play a saxophone?

Some dogs learn to skateboard from people, and others learn on their own. This dog loves it!

Some elephants like to paint pictures. How do you think they learned to be artists? What kinds of pictures do you paint?

Who is copying whom?

People have copied birds to learn how to fly. If birds could copy people, their babies might look like these babies. Could these baby birds learn to fly? Why or why not? Would they live in nests or in houses like humans? Write a story about these make-believe bird babies.

Learning more

Books

Kalman, Bobbie. *What is Super Nature?* (Big Science Ideas). Crabtree Publishing Company, 2011.

Kalman, Bobbie. *An animal community* (My World). Crabtree Publishing Company, 2010.

Taylor, Saranne. *Animal Homes* (Young Architect). Crabtree Publishing Company, 2015.

Lee, Dora. *Biomimicry: Inventions Inspired by Nature.* Kids Can Press, 2011.

Gates, Phil. *Nature Got There First* (Inventions Inspired by Nature). Kingfisher, 2010.

Websites

NASA: History of Flight: How did we learn to fly like the birds?
www.grc.nasa.gov/WWW/k-12/UEET/StudentSite/historyofflight.html

YouTube: Biomimicry: Design by Nature
www.youtube.com/watch?v=HPXYMBWjlks

NASA: Animals on the Move
http://spaceplace.nasa.gov/migration/en/#

Words to know

climate (KLAHY-mit) noun The normal, long-term weather conditions in an area

community (kuh-MYOO-ni-tee) noun A group of people or animals that live close together and help protect one another

glide (glahyd) verb To float on the wind smoothly without moving wings

habitat (HAB-i-tat) noun The natural area in which a plant or animal lives

keratin (KER-uh-tin) noun A tough substance that is found in hair, nails, and animal shells

predator (PRED-uh-tawr) noun An animal that hunts other animals for food

prey (prey) noun An animal that is hunted by another animal

protest (PROH-test) verb To oppose or object to something

shelter (SHEL-ter) noun Protection from bad weather or danger

wet suit (wet soot) noun A tight-fitting rubber suit that keeps a person's body warm in cold water

A noun is a person, place, or thing.
A verb is an action word that tells you what someone or something does.

Index